A READING GUIDE TO

A Wrinkle in Time

by Madeleine L'Engle

Manuela Soares

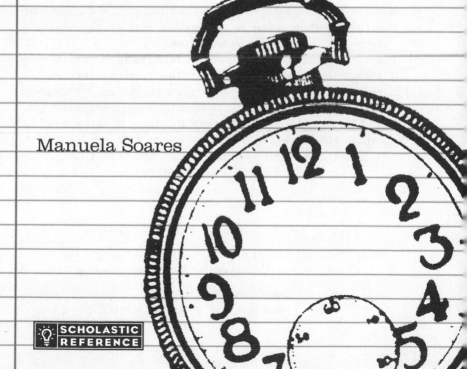

Library of Congress Cataloging-in-Publication Data
Soares, Manuela.
Scholastic BookFiles: A Reading Guide to A Wrinkle in Time by Madeleine L'Engle/by Manuela Soares.
p.   cm.
Summary: Discusses the writing, characters, plot, and themes of this 1963 Newbery Award–winning book. Includes discussion questions and activities.
Includes bibliographical references (p.).
1. L'Engle, Madeleine. A Wrinkle in Time—Juvenile literature.
2. Science fiction, American—History and criticism—Juvenile literature.   3. Space and time in literature—Juvenile literature.
[1. L'Engle, Madeleine. A Wrinkle in Time.   2. American literature—History and criticism.]   I. Title: A Reading Guide to A Wrinkle in Time by Madeleine L'Engle.   II. Title.
PS3523.E55W737 2003
813'.54—dc21   2002042665
0-439-46364-5

10 9 8 7 6 5 4 3 2 1   03 04 05 06 07

Composition by Brad Walrod/High Text Graphics, Inc.
Cover and interior design by Red Herring Design

Printed in the U.S.A.   23
First printing, July 2003

Contents

Madeleine L'Engle doesn't think of herself as a children's book writer. She's just a writer. She writes books that she would want to read.

L'Engle believes kids need heroes like Meg in *A Wrinkle in Time*, because heroes were important to her when she was growing up. "I always needed somebody that I wanted to be as good as," she says, "if not better than."

L'Engle was born Madeleine L'Engle Camp on November 29, 1918. Her mother was a pianist and her father was a journalist and a writer who fought in World War I. His lungs were damaged from mustard gas, a poisonous gas that was used as a weapon in the war. Because of his health problems, the family traveled to places where the air was dry and easy to breathe.

As an only child, L'Engle grew up lonely and always wished for a larger family. She says that's why the families in her novels have lots of children.

Wherever her parents lived they always had many friends— artists, musicians, and writers. "Their lives were very full and they really didn't have time for a child. So I turned to writing to amuse myself."

L'Engle grew up in a house full of books, so reading and writing came naturally. "My parents read aloud to each other every night," says L'Engle. Among the books they read were the works of the French writer Alexandre Dumas. It was from Dumas that L'Engle says she found "a sense of story."

When Madeleine was twelve, the family moved to a town in the French Alps. She was sent to a boarding school, which she hated. When she was fourteen, the family returned to the United States and Madeleine was sent to Ashley Hall, a boarding school in Ashley, South Carolina, which she loved. She was seventeen and still at Ashley Hall when her father died. She went on to spend four years at Smith College, graduating with honors in 1941. In 1981 Smith awarded her a Smith Medal for "service to the community that reflects the purpose of a liberal arts education."

After graduating from Smith, L'Engle moved to the Greenwich Village neighborhood in New York City with three other young women. She still wanted to be a writer, but "I had to pay the bills, so I went to work in the theater."

While she was on tour as an actress, Madeleine wrote her first book, *The Small Rain*. At this time she decided that having three names was more than she needed. So, Madeleine dropped her last name, Camp.

L'Engle knows all about her heritage. The name L'Engle can be traced back to two French brothers, one Catholic and one

Protestant. They fought and the Protestant brother got mad and left France. He changed the original spelling of his name, which was L'Angle, to L'Engle. "I'm descended from the mad brother!" L'Engle says with a laugh.

While she was rehearsing a play, she met an actor named Hugh Franklin. They were married when they were on tour with another play. A short time later, they both decided to give up acting. They moved to rural Connecticut, where they opened a general store.

"It was a very safe place to start raising our kids," L'Engle recalls. "No city lights, no noises at night." They lived in a very small town that is a lot like the town in *A Wrinkle in Time*. In fact, it was while they were living in Connecticut that L'Engle wrote *A Wrinkle in Time*.

Although their store was successful, the Franklins missed New York City. After ten years, they moved back to the city with their three children, settling into a large eight-room apartment overlooking the Hudson River.

Despite the fact that L'Engle was an author who had already published six books, it took more than two years to find a publisher for *A Wrinkle in Time*. Later, after the book was a success, one publisher who had rejected it told her, "I wish I'd had the chance to publish it." L'Engle mailed him a copy of the rejection slip he had sent her.

How does it feel to have such a huge success after trying for so long to find a publisher? "Since it was the book nobody wanted," says L'Engle, "it feels kind of nice."

A Wrinkle in Time won the prestigious Newbery Medal in 1963, the year after it was published. It is the first book in what became a four-book series called "The Time Quartet." Three other books about the Murry family were published after *A Wrinkle in Time*. They are *A Wind in the Door*, *A Swiftly Tilting Planet*, and *Many Waters*. In *A Wind in the Door*, Meg and Calvin, school principal Mr. Jenkins, a farandola, and a cherubim, travel inside one of Charles Wallace's mitochondria to save him from an evil being. In *A Swiftly Tilting Planet*, newly married Meg takes a telepathic trip with Charles Wallace through time in order to save the world once again. The twins Sandy and Dennys are the heroes in *Many Waters*, in which they time-travel to the time of the biblical Noah.

Another book, *An Acceptable Time,* is sometimes considered part of the Time series because it includes Meg's parents. But it is really about Polly O'Keefe, Meg's daughter. It belongs with the four-book series about the O'Keefe family, which also includes *The Arm of the Starfish*, *Dragons in the Water*, and *A House Like a Lotus*.

L'Engle's longest series is about the Austin family. The series has eight books: *The Twenty-Four Days Before Christmas*, *A Full House*, *Meet the Austins*, *The Anti-Muffins*, *The Moon by Night*, *The Young Unicorns*, *A Ring of Endless Light*, and *Troubling a Star*.

L'Engle has many personal heroes—people she looks to for inspiration and encouragement in her life and work. The composer Johann Sebastian Bach is high on her list. "If I get out of proportion and all confused, if I can sit down and play Bach fugues, he'll pull me back." She also loves Mozart and Scarlatti. L'Engle especially likes Albert Einstein and calls him "Saint Albert."

"He [Einstein] says that anyone who is not lost in rapture at the power of the mind behind the universe is as good as a burned out candle."

L'Engle has never lost her awe of the universe. This awe helps give her the inspiration to write.

"When I look at the night sky I'm looking at time as well as space," says the author, "looking at a star seven light-years away, and a star seventy light-years away.... It's so exciting that it makes me want to write ... so I send Meg to the outer galaxies."

Now in her mid-eighties, L'Engle is a writer-in-residence and a volunteer librarian at St. John the Divine Cathedral in New York City.

What advice does Madeleine L'Engle have for her readers?

"Be brave! Have courage! Don't fear! Do what you think you ought to do, even if it's nontraditional. Be open. Be ready to change."

Selected Awards

Below you will find a chronological list of the major awards Madeleine L'Engle has won during the course of her writing career.

- John Newbery Medal for *A Wrinkle in Time* (1963)
- Runner-Up, Hans Christian Andersen Award for *A Wrinkle in Time* (1964)
- Sequoyah Children's Book Award for *A Wrinkle in Time* (1965)
- Lewis Carroll Shelf Award for *A Wrinkle in Time* (1965)
- Austrian State Literary Prize for *The Moon by Night* (1969)
- Austrian State Literary Prize for *Camilla* (1971)
- Honor Certificate, New England Round Table of Children's Literature (1974)
- Newbery Honor Book Award for *A Ring of Endless Light* (1980)
- American Book Award for *A Swiftly Tilting Planet* (1980)
- Dorothy Canfield Fisher Children's Book Award for *A Ring of Endless Light* (1981)
- Newbery Honor Book Award for *A Swiftly Tilting Planet* (1981)
- Smith Medal from Smith College (1981)
- University of Southern Mississippi Silver Medallion for "outstanding contribution to the field of children's literature" (1986)
- ALAN Award for outstanding contribution to adolescent literature (1986)
- Margaret A. Edwards Award for "lifetime contribution to young adult literature" (1998)

Madeleine L'Engle had written and published several books before writing *A Wrinkle in Time*. Though L'Engle sent *Wrinkle* to many publishers, it kept getting rejected. "I got a few queries saying 'Who is the book for?' I said it's for people; I don't write for an age group, I write for people."

L'Engle explains further, "I write stories because that's how I look for truth. I was looking for truth when I was writing *Wrinkle*. We live in a world where it's very difficult for people to understand that a story can be truthful and not factual."

Most of the objections to the book, she recalls, "were that it would not be able to find an audience, that it was too difficult for children."

A Wrinkle in Time combines elements of science fiction and fantasy with two of L'Engle's special themes—moral responsibility and the power of love, especially family love. But it is also based on science, one of L'Engle's favorite subjects. She reads a lot of science books and uses scientific ideas in her writing.

In *Wrinkle*, tesseracts are used to travel through time and space. L'Engle says the science behind tesseracts is real. "I read a lot about particle physics and quantum mechanics, and I have a few scientist friends who will let me pick their brains. I came across the word 'tesseract' in a science article and kind of got fascinated by it."

Writers are always told to write about what they know, and L'Engle says she modeled the main character of Meg after herself, because "I'm the only person I know that well."

During her school life, L'Engle often felt as Meg does, lonely and awkward. She, too, had problems with her teachers. L'Engle also says she is stubborn, just like Meg. There are a few differences between Meg and the author, though. Meg is good in arithmetic and not so good in English. L'Engle was very good in English and didn't do so well in math.

L'Engle explains, "If I'm writing about a twelve- or fourteen-year-old, I've got to be myself at that age."

One question she is asked a lot is why she began the book with the words "It was a dark and stormy night. . . ." According to L'Engle, the phrase "a dark and stormy night" is one that is used to start lots of scary stories, the kind of stories people told around campfires when L'Engle was growing up. Those words let you know it is going to be a scary story.

When *Wrinkle* was finally published, L'Engle won the Newbery Medal, the most prestigious children's book award in America.

In her acceptance speech, she explained that the process of writing *A Wrinkle in Time* was a mysterious one:

> A writer of fantasy, fairy tale, or myth must inevitably discover that he is not writing out of his own knowledge or experience, but out of something both deeper and wider. I think that fantasy must possess the author and simply use him. I know that this is true of *A Wrinkle in Time*. I can't possibly tell you how I came to write it. It was simply a book I had to write. I had no choice. And it was only *after* it was written that I realized what some of it meant.

Chapter Charter:
Questions to Guide Your Reading

These questions will help you think about the important parts of each chapter.

Chapter 1

- What do Meg Murry's actions tell you about her? How does Meg feel about her family?
- How is Charles Wallace different from most five-year-olds? Have you ever met an unusual child like Charles Wallace?
- How do we know that Mrs. Whatsit is odd—but friendly?
- Does ending the chapter with the tessaract make you want to read on? If so, why?
- What does Mrs. Murry's treatment of Mrs. Whatsit tell you about Mrs. Murry?

Chapter 2

- Why does the school principal, Mr. Jenkins, want Meg to accept that her father is never coming home? Should Meg believe him? Why? Why not?
- In what ways are the twins Sandy and Dennys different from the rest of the Murry family?
- Why do the twins think Meg has so much trouble at school?
- What does Mrs. Who say to Meg that lets us know that something is about to happen?

Chapter 3

- How is Calvin's home life different from Meg's? How is his school life different from Meg's?
- What does Mrs. Murry mean when she says, "...just because we don't understand doesn't mean that the explanation doesn't exist."
- What is a "willing suspension of belief"? How does having a willing suspension of belief help Mrs. Murry?
- What are the hard questions that Calvin asks about Meg's father?
- Are you surprised when the children go off with Mrs. Who, Mrs. Whatsit, and Mrs. Which? Why do they go off with these strange women?

Chapter 4

- Why does Mrs. Who like to quote? Do you think it is an effective way to communicate with the children? Why or why not?
- Why do you think Calvin is asked to go on the journey with Megan and Charles Wallace?
- How would you react if you were taken on a surprise journey to another planet?

Chapter 5

- What does the children's experience in a two-dimensional planet tell you about tesser travel?
- During their journey, the children learn about the Dark Thing. What do you think the Dark Thing really is?
- Who are some of the famous people mentioned as fighting the Dark Thing? What do they all have in common?

Chapter 6

- Why is the Happy Medium's worst trouble "getting fond"?
- Describe the planet of Camazotz.
- What characters have you met through reading other books and stories who also have magical qualities like Mrs. Whatsit, Mrs. Who, and Mrs. Which?
- What do the children learn about the people of Camazotz? How do you know?

Chapter 7

- Charles Wallace says that they can't make decisions based on fear. Do you agree? Explain.
- When the man with red eyes tries to take over the children's minds, whom does Meg scream for and why?
- What mistake does Charles Wallace make when he meets the man with red eyes?

Chapter 8

- Charles Wallace seems well and happy, just as the man with red eyes says he is. How does Meg know that Charles Wallace's mind and heart have been taken over?
- Describe what life is like on Camazotz. How is it different from your own life? Is anything the same?
- How do they keep people from suffering on Camazotz? What do you think of this idea?
- What do you think IT is?

Chapter 9

- Why does Charles Wallace want to take Mrs. Who's spectacles from Meg?

- Do you believe, as Meg does, that Mr. Murry will really save them? Why or why not?
- Explain the phrase "like and equal are two entirely different things." How does this idea help Meg?

Chapter 10
- Why is Meg so sick after escaping from IT?
- What are Meg's feelings about her father, brother, and Calvin after escaping from IT? Do you think she should feel this way? Explain why.
- What do you think of Mr. Murry's reasons for not rescuing Charles Wallace? Do you agree with him? Why or why not?

Chapter 11
- What would you do if you suddenly met three aliens?
- What is it about the beast that convinces Meg to trust her? What are some of the things that let you trust someone?
- Why do you think Meg finally trusts the beast?
- Why is the name Aunt Beast a good one for this alien creature?
- Why do the time travelers have so much trouble explaining Mrs. Whatsit to the creatures on Ixchel?

Chapter 12
- Why doesn't Meg hug Mrs. Whatsit when she appears on Ixchel?
- Why does Meg have to be the one to go after Charles Wallace?
- How does Mr. Murry help Meg on the journey back to Camazotz?
- What gift does Mrs. Whatsit give Meg for her journey back to Camazotz? What is Mrs. Which's gift?
- What does Meg have that IT doesn't have? Is this something she can use in other situations? If so, how?

"What could there be about a shadow that was so terrible that she knew that there had never been before or ever would be again, anything that would chill her with a fear that was beyond shuddering, beyond crying or screaming, beyond the possibility of comfort."

—*A Wrinkle in Time*

A *Wrinkle in Time* is about the journey of three children to find a missing man, and perhaps help save the universe.

Twelve-year-old Meg Murry is having problems at school. She is bored with schoolwork and doesn't seem to fit in with the other kids. Meg has ten-year-old twin brothers, Sandy and Dennys, but she's closest with her five-year-old brother, Charles Wallace.

Meg's father has been missing for some time, and she is worried about him. Some people think that Mr. Murry abandoned the family. But Meg and her mother believe that Mr. Murry is doing important government work and, for some unknown reason, can't return to them.

Charles Wallace has made friends with a very odd lady, Mrs. Whatsit. One evening, Charles Wallace and Meg go to visit Mrs. Whatsit and her two friends, Mrs. Who and Mrs. Which. The children find an older boy, Calvin O'Keefe, near the house. Meg recognizes Calvin from school. After visiting the ladies, the children go back to the Murry house for dinner where Calvin and Meg get to know each other better. Before the night is over, Charles Wallace tells them that Mrs. Who, Mrs. Whatsit, and Mrs. Which are taking them on a trip to an unkown location.

"I don't know [where] exactly," says Charles Wallace. "But I think it's to find Father."

It's a scary trip because Meg finds herself completely and utterly alone in soundless darkness. When they arrive at their first destination, the planet Uriel, Meg discovers that they have tessered—or wrinkled—through time.

Mrs. Whatsit transforms into a white horselike creature and flies the children to a mountaintop on the planet Uriel. There she shows the children what they are fighting: a dark thing that blots out all light. It is so huge it can surround planets—including Earth. This dark thing makes everyone shudder with fear. They also learn that Mr. Murry has been fighting the Dark Thing (also called the Black Thing). To rescue him, the children will have to travel behind the Dark Thing to the planet Camazotz. Their three guardians will be able to watch, but they will not be able to do anything to help the children.

On Camazotz, Calvin, Charles Wallace, and Meg find a town where all the houses look the same. In identical front yards, children are bouncing balls and skipping rope in unison. Each ball and rope hits the sidewalk at the exact same instant. The doors to each house open at the same time, and mothers come out at the same moment. The paperboy comes by, throwing the paper to exactly the same spot at every house. He tells the children that this is the capital of Camazotz: "Our factories never close; our machines never stop rolling. . . . We are the most oriented city on the planet. There has been no trouble of any kind for centuries. All Camazotz knows our record. That is why CENTRAL Central Intelligence is located here. That is why IT makes ITs home here."

Calvin, Charles Wallace, and Meg admit to being very afraid, but that doesn't stop them from going to the huge CENTRAL Central Intelligence Building. They are taken into a room where they find the man with red eyes, who communicates without using words. He tries to hypnotize them, but the children resist. Eventually, he succeeds in taking over Charles Wallace's mind.

The children are taken to see Mr. Murry, who is trapped in a tall transparent column. Charles Wallace tells Meg that the only way to save Mr. Murry is if she gives in to IT. At the mention of IT, Meg's skin crawls and she knows that IT is the Dark Thing, the thing that has captured Charles Wallace and her father.

Before Charles Wallace can stop her, Meg runs through the transparent glass wall and joins her father in the column. Mr. Murry is able to leave the column with Meg in his arms.

When Charles Wallace insists that they go to see IT, Mr. Murry agrees. Meg is frightened. She can feel a rhythmic pulsing coming from the building, like it was breathing for her, taking her breath away. They enter the building and are taken to a room where— lying on a dais—is a brain, an oversized, disembodied brain! IT!

Meg tries to resist IT's pulsing power. She fights to stay conscious, but can't hold out against IT and loses consciousness. As Meg slowly comes to her senses, she feels awfully cold and can't move or speak. While she can hear Calvin and Mr. Murry talking, she can't signal them in any way. She discovers they are on another planet having escaped IT—but they've left Charles Wallace behind.

Suddenly three alien figures walk toward them. They are large and gray with four arms and more than five waving tentacles on each hand. Their furry faces are featureless, with only indentations where an Earthling would have eyes, a nose, and a mouth.

When the smallest alien bends over her, suddenly Meg feels peaceful and sleepy. The aliens inform Mr. Murry that Meg, burned by the coldness of the Black Thing, is in grave danger. Mr. Murry and Calvin can't save her, but the alien creatures can. When Meg wakes up, she feels much better. The pain and cold she felt is now just a memory. Meg calls her creature friend Aunt Beast.

The three Mrs. Ws reappear and discuss what can be done to rescue Charles Wallace from Camazotz. They say the only person who can do it is Meg. She must face IT all by herself. Meg is very frightened—the Dark Thing almost got her once! But she agrees to go.

Back on Camazotz, Meg finds Charles Wallace and tries to talk to him. Meanwhile, IT attempts to take over her mind again. Meg lets all the love inside her heart flow out to her young brother. She looks Charles Wallace in the eye and repeats to herself, I love you I love you I love you. Suddenly, the real Charles Wallace is back! He races to Meg, and in a flash they are whisked away from Camazotz by Mrs. Whatsit. In seconds, they tumble across the lawn at home. Charles Wallace clings to Meg. "You saved me! You saved me!" Mr. Murry and Calvin are there, too, both safe at home.

Thinking about the plot

- Dangerous things happen throughout the story. How does this create suspense?
- Why is it so important for the children to stay together?
- What is the most important thing that happens to each of the children?
- Are Meg, Calvin, and Charles Wallace changed by what happens to them? How?

"Oh, no! We can't stop here! This is a
two-dimensional planet and the
children can't manage here!"

—A Wrinkle in Time

At the beginning of *A Wrinkle in Time*, the reader might think they're going to stay in Meg's town for the entire story. But there are many different settings in the book, mostly alien.

When the story opens, Meg Murry is awake in her attic bedroom listening to a storm. The Murry family lives in a big old house, which the author describes as Meg goes down to the kitchen for some warm milk to help her sleep. Her room in the attic is small. The rest of the attic is much larger and has a Ping-Pong table, a rocking horse, an old dolls' house, and an electric train set. On the second floor there are three bedrooms for her parents and brothers. A big old-fashioned kitchen is on the first floor. Off this kitchen are a pantry, a garage, and an old stone dairy that Mrs. Murry uses as her scientific lab.

The kitchen is cheerful, with curtains, flowers blooming on the windowsills, and a bouquet of flowers on the table. Though the windows were rattling in the attic and the wind was howling through the chimneys, Meg feels safe and warm in the kitchen. Even though Meg is sometimes upset and unhappy, her family's home gives her comfort and security.

The house used to be the Murrys' vacation home. But now, since Meg's father has disappeared, they live there permanently. The house is about four miles away from the village where the children go to school.

This comfortable and very quiet community, never named, could be almost anywhere in America. It's the kind of town where the biggest excitement is that someone has taken sheets from a neighbor's clothesline. It is also a gossipy town where people say that Mr. Murry has deserted the family and is never coming back.

Life begins to get strange when three very odd ladies—Mrs. Whatsit, Mrs. Which, and Mrs. Who—quietly move into the abandoned house in the pine woods behind the Murry property. Soon after meeting the ladies, Meg, Calvin, and Charles Wallace find themselves in a very different setting. The three Mrs. Ws have taken them to Uriel, the third planet of the star Malak in the spiral nebula Messier 101.

They land in a field filled with flowers and sunlight. It is enough like Earth for Calvin to wonder if they are still on their own planet. But as the travelers explore, it's clear that this isn't Earth. They travel across a plain filled with large granite monoliths set in rhythmic patterns. They continue on, passing over a garden that is "more beautiful than anything in a dream."

By a crystal-clear river, they find many white horselike creatures with rainbow wings—like Mrs. Whatsit. These magical creatures make music that fills the children with awe and joy. These alien beings and their music show us that this is another place, definitely not planet Earth.

The children each receive a flower that has hundreds of tiny blossoms. With these flowers, they can breathe when Mrs. Whatsit takes them up into the thinning atmosphere. As one of Uriel's moons is setting, the children see a huge black cloud in space. It is a shadow that hides the stars and allows no light to shine through. Looking at it, the children know it is evil, dark, and dreadful.

When they return to the flowery field, Uriel's smaller moon is rising, bathing everything in a lovely, golden glow. Seeing a moon that reminds the children of Earth is a comfort after the dread of the Dark Thing.

The next location in the book is a two-dimensional planet where they can't breathe. Meg "felt a pressure she had never imagined, as though she were being completely flattened out by an enormous steam roller."

The next setting is more obviously alien than Uriel. The children land in Orion's Belt to visit the Happy Medium. The atmosphere is foggy and they are standing on a flat gray surface. They can't see anything except one another. As they walk, they realize that there are no trees or bushes, just an occasional rock. The Happy Medium lives in a big stone cave.

Their final stop in the search for Mr. Murry is Camazotz, a planet taken over by the Dark Thing. The odd thing about Camazotz is that it looks just like Earth. It has the same kind of hills and trees and grass. Even the creatures living on Camazotz look like humans. The big difference is that they don't behave the way people do on Earth. The fact that Camazotz is so much like Earth, yet so alien, makes it extremely frightening.

On Camazotz, the children wander through the main city. They stop and look at the houses and the people. They walk to the CENTRAL Central Intelligence Building, where they find Mr. Murry. Eventually, they are taken to a domelike building that houses IT.

In trying to escape from IT, Mr. Murry, who is inexperienced with tessering, accidentally takes them to Ixchel. This place is in the same solar system as Camazotz, but it is very different. Ixchel is the strangest planet by far. It has brown grass and trees and gray flowers. Even the tall creatures that inhabit the planet are gray. There is a wonderful scent in the air.

The author establishes the differences between the inhabitants of Ixchel and humans by having Meg and Aunt Beast talk about how different "seeing" is for each of them.

After Meg's brief return to Camazotz to rescue Charles Wallace, the children are back on Earth with Mr. Murry within minutes of having left. Meg, Charles Wallace, and Calvin return from their adventures in time and space without anyone else noticing they were gone. The familiar smells and sounds of Earth and the fall season are all there to welcome them home.

Thinking about the setting

- How do the different planets and places the children visit add to the story?
- If you could pick another world for the children to travel to, what would it be like? And why?
- Which of the settings did you like the most? If you had the opportunity to move there, would you? Why or why not?

"The light spread out and where it touched the Darkness the Darkness disappeared. The light spread until the patch of Dark Thing had vanished, and there was only a gentle shining, and through the shining came the stars, clear and pure."

—*A Wrinkle in Time*

There are many themes in *A Wrinkle in Time*, but the major theme is the struggle of good versus evil. This struggle takes place not only on the planet Earth, but throughout the universe. Love is the strongest weapon in the fight against evil. And this is the other most prominent theme—the power of love, in families and among friends, to fight evil. Two other themes are faith and trust—Meg's faith that her father will return to the family and that everything will work out; and trust between the children and the three ladies. The children trust the three ladies to help them and guide them and keep them safe in the same way they rely on their parents.

Daring to be different is another theme. In their own ways, Meg, Charles Wallace, and Calvin are very different from the other kids they know. Those differences make life harder for each of them, but they still have to be true to themselves. To be able to do this takes courage, another theme of the book. The children show courage when they fight against evil even though they're afraid. In fighting against evil, they use everything—including their own faults. Using our faults is another theme. Understanding how to use their faults to accomplish good helps the children in their struggle against evil.

Good versus evil and love versus hate

The primary theme of the book is about the battle between good and evil. According to the author, the forces of darkness and those of light have been fighting each other since time began. Darkness is the absence of light. When a person is "in the dark" about something, it's a way of saying that they don't know what's going on. Without light, nothing can be seen and nothing can grow. The evil in Camazotz blocks out all love, and as a result, the people are frightened and unhappy.

The three ladies tell the children that their planet, Earth, has always had some of the very best fighters against evil and the powers of darkness. Jesus is named as well as Gandhi and Buddha, Einstein, Bach, and Pasteur, among others.

Madeleine L'Engle believes that the way to fight darkness and evil is through light and love. For L'Engle and her characters in *A Wrinkle in Time*, love saves the day.

Love

How is love shown in *A Wrinkle in Time*? There is the love between Mr. and Mrs. Murry and their children. This is the love that draws Calvin to Meg and her family. There is the special love Meg and her little brother Charles Wallace feel for each other. There is also the love between Calvin and Meg.

Love is a very powerful force in this book. Meg and Charles Wallace undertake the dangerous journey to rescue their father because their love for him is so strong. The love between Aunt Beast and Meg is what allows Meg to heal from passing through the Black Thing. Meg's love for Charles Wallace sends her back alone to Camazotz to rescue him. It is the love of Aunt Beast and the three ladies, as well as her parents, that helps Meg rescue Charles Wallace. And it is Charles Wallace's love for Meg that brings him out of his trance so he can escape IT. The story ends on a positive note because love triumphs over every obstacle or problem.

Faith

Faith is accepting things without understanding them completely. It's not always possible to understand everything; some things just have to be taken on faith. *A Wrinkle in Time* is a novel with many examples of practicing faith.

Meg struggles to believe her father is coming home, yet she's afraid that he never will. Mrs. Murry, Meg's mother, believes that her husband will return. It is Mrs. Murry's faith that keeps Meg's faith alive.

There are other examples of having faith. Each time the children "tesser"—that is, travel through time and space—they are putting their faith in the three ladies who are their guides. They believe their guides will keep them safe as they travel. The children also believe that they can find and rescue Mr. Murry. If they didn't have faith that they could do that, they wouldn't have tried.

The three "guardian angels"—Mrs. Whatsit, Mrs. Who, and Mrs. Which—also have faith. Their faith is that the children can succeed against the Black Thing and save Mr. Murry.

All of the characters on the side of good in *A Wrinkle in Time* have faith that love will triumph over evil.

Trust

Trust is having confidence in someone because of their strength or knowledge or ability. Calvin and Meg trust Charles Wallace, who is barely five. They trust his judgment because he knows and understands things they don't. Meg and Calvin trust Mrs. Whatsit, Mrs. Who, and Mrs. Which even though they are strangers because Charles Wallace has confidence in them.

Calvin and Meg and Charles Wallace also have to trust one another and have faith in one another's abilities as they journey through time and space.

Growing up, Meg thought that her father could fix everything, and she had complete trust in him. Toward the end of the story, Meg realizes that her father makes mistakes and doesn't always make decisions that she agrees with. Realizing that he isn't perfect destroys her trust in him for a while. When she finally understands that no one can fix everything, she learns a valuable lesson. She understands that what she can trust about her father is his love for her.

Daring to be different

All three main characters—Meg, Calvin, and Charles Wallace— are kids who don't quite fit in because they are different in some way. These differences make Calvin and Meg unhappy. Meg doesn't fit in at school but has a great family life. Calvin fits in well at school but not at home.

Meg doesn't fit in because, though she loves math, she doesn't do it the way her teachers do. This makes her unhappy at school because it means she's not like everybody else. Calvin fits in at school; his athletic ability makes him popular and accepted by other students. But at home, he doesn't fit in because he's not like the rest of his family.

Charles Wallace, who hasn't started school, understands that to be different can mean being unhappy. He pretends not to be smart so he will be accepted by the other kids when he gets to school.

Being different can be lonely. But would it be any better if everyone were the same? The problem on Camazotz is that everyone has to be exactly alike. They must conform. Conforming to what other people expect of you means changing yourself to fit in. It means being like everybody else.

"Differences create problems," says IT through the hypnotized Charles Wallace. And so on Camazotz, IT makes everyone exactly the same. IT robs people of their choices, their ability to be different.

When faced with IT on Camazotz, Meg says: "I am willing to assume all the pain, all the responsibility, all the burdens of thought and decision. . . ." Because even though Meg doesn't like being different, "I don't want to be like everybody else, either."

Even if it makes them unhappy sometimes, Meg, Calvin, and Charles Wallace have to be themselves.

Courage

Courage is having the strength to resist and endure fear, danger, and difficulty. It takes a lot of courage for Calvin, Meg, and Charles Wallace to travel to other worlds by themselves. They must face a lot of terrible beings—the Black Thing, the man with red eyes, the evil brain known as IT. But that doesn't mean they are not afraid. Don't be afraid to be afraid because "only a fool is not afraid," Mrs. Whatsit tells them. There is great danger in going behind the Black Thing, but the children still go, which takes great courage.

There are many examples of courage in *A Wrinkle in Time*. Mrs. Whatsit was once a star who was not afraid to battle the Black Thing. She won the battle, but she paid a terrible price—she is no longer a star. Mrs. Murry has courage, too. She resists the fear that her husband won't return. Her courage inspires her children to believe that Mr. Murry will return—and to search for him when they have the chance. Meg shows amazing courage when she agrees to go back to Camazotz for Charles Wallace— even after suffering terrible pain as a result of her first encounter with IT.

Using our faults

This book is also about faults—character flaws such as anger and impatience in Meg and pride and arrogance in Charles Wallace. But instead of completely condemning faults, Mrs. Whatsit tells Meg, "I give you your faults"—which she says might help Meg on Camazotz. Meg doesn't understand this. "But I'm always trying to get rid of my faults," she protests.

So are faults helpful or not? Are they things we should get rid of? Try to control? Or are they things we have to understand about ourselves and use in more positive ways? Meg's anger is a good example. It's not good to be angry, but Meg's anger helps her to fight her fear. When she's angry, she doesn't feel so afraid.

In Chapter 6, Mrs. Whatsit says that the danger is greatest for Charles Wallace because he's the most vulnerable. "Beware of pride and arrogance, Charles, for they may betray you." And in fact, they do; his overconfidence in his abilities allows IT to take over his mind and body. But Charles Wallace's pride in his abilities is also an important tool for him. It allows him to try things that he might not otherwise have the courage to do.

Thinking about the themes

- How are Mr. Murry's actions examples of the themes in the book?
- How important do you think love is in the world? Is it more important to love or be loved?
- How does love save Charles Wallace?
- What is so evil about IT?

"What have I got that IT hasn't got?"

—Meg, *A Wrinkle in Time*

Though this is primarily a story about Meg, Charles Wallace, and Calvin, there are many other characters in the book. Some make only brief appearances while others come and go throughout the story.

Here is a list of the major characters, followed by descriptions of each one.

Main characters

In order of appearance:

Meg Murry	a twelve-year-old girl
Charles Wallace Murry	Meg's five-year-old brother
Mrs. Murry	Meg's mother
Mrs. Whatsit	a strange neighbor
Sandy and Dennys Murry	Meg's ten-year-old twin brothers
Calvin O'Keefe	a fourteen-year-old boy
Mrs. Who	a strange neighbor
Mrs. Which	a strange neighbor
the man with red eyes	man possessed by IT

Mr. Murry	Meg's father
IT	an evil alien being, the Boss
Aunt Beast	a good alien being

Meg Murry: Mcg is a twelve-year-old girl who is fiercely loyal and protective of her family and is especially attached to her little brother, Charles Wallace. When Meg is feeling sad or lonely, she tells herself, "Charles loves me at any rate." She worries about Charles Wallace not being able to fit in when he goes to school next year. Both of them are very, very smart and that sets them apart from other kids. Meg wears glasses and loves math.

Meg has heard people talking about her family: "The two boys seem to be nice, regular children, but that unattractive girl and the baby boy certainly aren't all there." Comments like this make her angry.

Meg is very familiar with her faults—impatience and anger are high on the list. She's also very stubborn. She tries hard to control her emotions, but she often doesn't succeed.

Meg's father, Mr. Murry, has been missing for quite some time and she's angry and upset about it. Meg misses him terribly. She doesn't know what has happened to him, and there seems to be nothing she can do.

Meg doesn't fit in at school, where she can't seem to do anything right. She is lonely and unhappy until Calvin comes along. Calvin seems to understand and like her, and she likes him, too. Once she and Calvin and Charles Wallace go off with Mrs. Whatsit,

Mrs. Who, and Mrs. Which, Meg matures a great deal. She discovers that finally there is something she can do for her father.

Meg is very focused on helping her father. More than Calvin and Charles Wallace, Meg never forgets that he's the reason behind their journey. Her impatience shows in her eagerness to find him and her anger at anything that delays them. "Meg was in such an agony of impatience that her voice grated irritably. '. . . But what about Father? Please, what about Father,' she pleads with the Mrs. Ws."

Throughout the journey, Meg remains a loyal friend to Calvin and a loving sister to Charles Wallace.

Charles Wallace: Meg's five-year-old brother is a very special little boy. He knows things without being told, and he understands things that most five-year-olds wouldn't. Charles Wallace is always adding words to his vocabulary. He enunciates clearly, like a much older child. It becomes clear early in the story that Charles Wallace is a genius. Yet people think he's a moron because he doesn't speak often. He's also a realist: "I think it will be better," Charles Wallace tells Meg, "if people go on thinking I'm not very bright. They won't hate me quite so much."

When Meg asks Charles Wallace if he can read minds, he lets her know that he understands things that other people cannot. He says he's "able to understand a sort of language, like sometimes if I concentrate very hard I can understand the wind talking with the trees."

Charles Wallace can even understand Mrs. Whatsit, Mrs. Which, and Mrs. Who. It's Charles Wallace who first makes friends with them. And it is Charles Wallace who persuades Meg and Calvin to trust the three ladies and go with them to find Mr. Murry.

Charles Wallace loves his older sister, Meg, and tries to take care of her. He makes sure she knows that he loves her. He understands Meg in a way that no one else can—or could until Calvin comes along.

Despite being so intelligent, Charles Wallace does have faults. Mrs. Whatsit warns him to beware of pride and arrogance. For example, he is convinced he can protect Meg no matter what. When Mrs. Whatsit tells Calvin to take care of her, Charles Wallace says rather sharply, "I can take care of Meg. I always have."

Sometimes he puts too much trust in his own abilities. Mrs. Who says to him, "Remember that you do not know everything." Charles Wallace doesn't remember and he ends up under IT's control.

Mrs. Murry: Meg's mother is a beautiful woman with doctoral degrees in biology and bacteriology. Mrs. Murry hasn't given up hope that her husband will return. She tells Calvin that she's been working on an experiment "so I won't be too far behind my husband when he gets back."

When she is with her children, Mrs. Murry seems calm and capable. But she's also honest with Meg about how upset she is about her husband's disappearance. She's clearly a great mother because she defends her children. She lets Meg know that she loves her no matter what. Mrs. Murry is confident that Meg will grow up to be as beautiful as she is even though Meg doesn't believe it herself.

Mrs. Murry is smart about all of her children. She knows that Charles Wallace is different, but she also knows that while she can help Meg and Charles Wallace with practical things, in the end they have to make their own way in the world. She believes they are smart enough to do it.

Mrs. Whatsit: Mrs. Whatsit is a strange neighbor who appears at the Murry house looking like a smallish tramp completely bundled up in clothes, including a shocking pink stole knotted around an overcoat, and black rubber boots. She has several scarves of assorted colors tied around her head with a man's felt hat perched on top and "a voice like an unoiled gate."

But even this decidedly odd person finds hospitality in the Murry household. Meg makes her a sandwich and Mrs. Murry helps Mrs. Whatsit take off her wet boots. Mrs. Whatsit praises Mrs. Murry for letting Charles Wallace be himself. She upsets Mrs. Murry as she's leaving by mentioning tesseracts.

Mrs. Whatsit is the youngest of the three ladies whom Calvin calls the "guardian angels." She is the one with the most human qualities. She is also the one closest to the children. We see Mrs. Whatsit in her real form—as a strange and beautiful white horselike creature—on the planet Uriel. We learn that she used to be a real light-emitting star before the Black Thing took over. Despite all she has suffered, she still has hope that the Black Thing can be overcome.

Sandy and Dennys Murry: Meg's ten-year-old twin brothers are fiercely independent and self-sufficient. The twins don't feature prominently in this book, but they serve a purpose: They are ordinary kids and contrast with Meg and Charles Wallace, each of whom is unusual.

The twins clearly don't have problems fitting in, and they're critical of Meg for not doing better in school.

"I wish you wouldn't be such a *dope*, Meg," says Sandy. "Use a happy *medium*, for heaven's sake. You just goof around in school and look out the window and don't pay any attention."

"You just make things harder for yourself," says Dennys.

They also worry that Charles Wallace is going to be just like Meg when he gets to school. But the twins are also very protective of their siblings and offer to defend Meg and Charles Wallace at any time.

Calvin O'Keefe: Calvin is a poorly dressed fourteen-year-old boy from a large family. "Tall he certainly was, and skinny. His bony wrists stuck out of the sleeves of his blue sweater; his worn corduroy trousers were three inches too short. He had orange hair that needed cutting and the appropriate freckles to go with it. His eyes were an oddly bright blue."

Calvin is athletic and popular at school. Like Meg, Calvin is unhappy, but his unhappiness comes from his home life, not his school life. When he first meets Meg and Charles Wallace in the woods, Calvin tells them that he's there to get away from his family. He is the third of eleven children. He feels different from the rest of his family. His mother and his siblings don't really care about him. He tells Meg, "You don't know how lucky you are to be loved."

Like Charles Wallace, who understands things without being told, Calvin has special talents, too. Calvin confesses that he gets "compulsions" and that he always does what his strange feelings tell him to do.

Calvin feels close to Meg and Charles Wallace right away. When Charles Wallace invites him to dinner, Calvin says, "I've never even seen your house, and I have the funniest feeling that for the first time in my life I'm going home!" Calvin gets along very well with Mrs. Murry, too, and even impresses the twins because he's a sports star at school. But it's Meg he cares about.

In Chapter 3, Calvin really wants to know about Meg, so he asks her a lot of questions about her father and what has happened to him. He repeats the only story he knows about Mr. Murry—"he's supposed to have left your mother and gone off with some dame." Meg jumps up, ready for a fight, but Calvin calms her down. "*You* know it isn't true, *I* know it isn't true."

He also asks her these questions because he wants Meg to be able to talk about all of her doubts and fears. Calvin isn't afraid of her anger or her tears. He lets her cry and encourages her to be herself.

Throughout the book, Calvin frequently takes Meg's hand or puts his arm protectively around her. He's always worried about Meg and looks out for her.

Mrs. Who: Mrs. Who is a plump little woman with enormous eyeglasses "twice as thick and twice as large as Meg's." She is one of the three "guardian angels" in the book. She loves to use quotes to make her point. As Mrs. Whatsit explains: "She finds it so difficult to verbalize. . . . It helps her if she can quote instead of working out words of her own."

And she stands up for Calvin, saying to Charles Wallace, "He wasn't my idea, Charlsie, but I think he's a good one."

Mrs. Who gives Meg her eyeglasses to help rescue Mr. Murry from IT. She also gives advice to each of the children before they go to Camazotz. At the end of the book, she recites a long quote to inspire Meg and guide her on her mission to rescue Charles Wallace on Camazotz.

Mrs. Which: She is the eldest and the leader of the trio of ladies who escort the children into the unknown. Mrs. Which is a shadow, hardly seen, but very much there.

It is Mrs. Which who says, "I ddo nott thinkk I willl matterrialize commpletely. I ffindd itt verry ttirinngg, andd wee hhave mmuch ttoo ddoo."

Mrs. Which is the wisest and the most powerful of the three "guardian angels," and not as friendly as Mrs. Whatsit and Mrs. Who. She knows more than the other two ladies. Mrs. Whatsit says that Mrs. Which hardly ever makes a mistake. Mrs. Which worries that the children will be frightened and warns Mrs. Whatsit about telling them too much.

Mrs. Which doesn't want to waste time letting the Happy Medium show the children scenes from home. She knows it will upset them—and she is right.

It is Mrs. Which who gives the children the command to go into the town on Camazotz and not to become separated no matter what. She is also the one who takes Meg back, alone, to rescue Charles Wallace.

The man with red eyes: The man with red eyes lives on Camazotz. He has been taken over by IT. He speaks for IT, just as Charles Wallace does when he is taken over. The man with red eyes also calls himself the Prime Coordinator.

His voice is kind and gentle, but his eyes are a horrible fiery red. He doesn't need to speak out loud because the children can hear him anyway. He tries to hypnotize Meg, Charles Wallace, and Calvin and take over their minds. He tries to persuade them to give in, telling them that he doesn't have to use violence, that there are other ways to take them over. He even threatens the children with starvation.

The man with red eyes is not trustworthy. He lies and he threatens until he finally persuades Charles Wallace to look deep into his eyes. Once he has taken over Charles Wallace, he uses the boy to take Calvin and Meg to Mr. Murry. He has to use Charles Wallace because the man with red eyes can never leave the room he is in.

Mr. Murry: When the story begins, Meg's father has been missing for a long time. He is a physicist who had been working for the government. No one knows for sure where he is, but his family believes that he is on a dangerous and secret mission.

When we finally meet Mr. Murry, he is trapped in a transparent column on Camazotz, trying to resist IT. His first thought is for Meg. He wants her to save herself, not him. When he realizes that Mrs. Who's glasses can free them both, he takes Meg into his arms and escapes from the column with her.

Mr. Murry tries to help Meg resist IT by telling her to think of the periodic table of elements and the square roots of numbers. Finally, he tessers Calvin and Meg away from Camazotz. He knows that Meg is upset and unhappy about leaving Charles Wallace behind on Camazotz, but it is the best he can do.

He tries to be patient with Meg. He tells her, "I am a human being, and a very fallible one. But I agree with Calvin. We were sent here for something. And we know that all things work together for good to them that love God, to them who are the called according to his purpose."

Mr. Murry is very protective of Meg, yet he allows her to make her own decisions. He doesn't let the creatures on Ixchel take his daughter away until he's convinced that they are going to help her. Later, when everyone understands that only Meg can save Charles Wallace, Mr. Murry doesn't want her to go back to Camazotz. He realizes that even though he wants to do everything for Meg, he can't fix all the hurts or right all the wrongs or bear her pain for her.

When Mr. Murry finally accepts that Meg must go back to Camazotz alone to rescue Charles Wallace, he lets her go.

"You are going to allow Meg the privilege of accepting this danger. You are a wise man, Mr. Murry," says Mrs. Whatsit.

IT: IT is a disembodied alien brain. "An oversized brain, just enough larger than normal to be completely revolting and terrifying . . . a brain that pulsed and quivered, that seized and commanded." This is the power behind the man with red eyes. This is the Black Thing, the evil shadow that takes over planets and people and deadens whatever it touches.

Aunt Beast: Aunt Beast is a very, very tall gray being with four arms and lots of long waving tentacles at the end of each one. She first meets Meg when she and two friends greet the newcomers to their planet, Ixchel. These creatures have only indentations where a human would have features like a nose, mouth, and eyes. Their entire bodies are covered with the softest fur imaginable, and they give off a beautiful smell.

Aunt Beast heals Meg from the effects of IT. She doesn't communicate the way we do; instead, she talks through the tentacles in her fingers. She doesn't "see" like humans do, either. Nonetheless, Meg and Aunt Beast understand each other as if they were mother and child. Aunt Beast takes care of the helpless Meg as though she were a baby. She bathes her, feeds her, and clothes her.

Aunt Beast talks to Meg, trying to reassure her at first, and then trying to explain her world to Meg and to understand Meg's own world.

Thinking about the characters
• How does Charles Wallace get trapped by IT?
• How are the beings different on each of the planets that the children visit? How would you describe them? How are they different from people on Earth?
• What do Mrs. Who's quotations tell us about her? Do the quotations give you any clues about what is going to happen next? Can you think of an example?

An award-winner

This Newbery Medal winner was published in 1962. More than ten million copies of this famous novel have been sold since then.

A Wrinkle in Time is beloved by both children and adults. The children's librarians of the American Librarian Association thought it was so good they named it a Notable Book for Children. Book reviewers also were impressed with L'Engle's work. A reviewer from the *Saturday Review* wrote that it "is original, different, exciting." Another reviewer, this one from *The New York Times Book Review,* described the novel in this way: "Imaginative readers should find it wholly absorbing—for in her highly accelerated spin through space, Miss L'Engle never loses sight of human needs and emotions."

In fact, so many people of all ages enjoyed the book *A Wrinkle in Time* that a television mini-series is being developed. No airdate has been decided so far, but keep an eye peeled for Meg, Charles Wallace, and Calvin to appear on the small screen soon.

Ban this book?

Although *A Wrinkle in Time* is on many children's (and adults') favorite books lists, not everyone loves it. *A Wrinkle in Time* is on several "banned books" lists. This means that some people don't think the book should be read—by anyone—and they have challenged the book being included in their library. According to the American Library Association, "A challenge is an attempt to remove or restrict materials based upon the objections of a person or group. A banning is the removal of those materials."

Why does this book provoke such strong feelings? *A Wrinkle in Time* has been banned by various religious groups that feel the book undermines religious beliefs. Some critics claim that the book challenges their idea of God. (If you remember, L'Engle uses some biblical references in the novel.) Some people think it's too Christian, while others think it is not Christian enough.

Although Madeleine L'Engle is a Christian, she doesn't feel that any of her books have specific Christian messages. She doesn't want to limit her books to Christians readers. If her books have any message, says L'Engle, it's that "the universe is basically benign [harmless]."

Here are some words that are used in *A Wrinkle in Time.* Knowing what these words mean will help you better understand the novel.

apprehension a fear or worry about something in the future

authoritative official; coming from someone who has the power to give orders

belligerent eager to fight; hostile

bravado an act or pretense of being brave

compulsion an irresistible desire to do something

constraint something that limits what you are able or allowed to do

corporeal substantial; having a physical or material body

diastole something that opens regularly, like a heart valve

dilapidated shabby and falling to pieces

disembodied seeming not to come from a person or thing

dissolution the act or process of disappearing or ending

dwindle to become smaller or less

elliptic roundabout; vague

ephemeral lasting a very short time

extinguish to put out (as in a fire); to put an end to

inadvertently not meaning to

indentation a depression or hollow in a surface

indignation anger aroused by someone or something unworthy, unjust, or mean

ineffable not able to be described in words

inexorable inflexible; not able to be persuaded

malignant dangerous because it tends to spread and eventually cause death

materialize to appear; to become real

metamorphose to change into a different form

miasma an atmosphere or vapor that hides things or spoils them

omnipotent having unlimited authority

prodigious amazing or wonderful; very big

protoplasm the jellylike living matter of most plant and animal cells

radiance a state or quality of being bright and shining

resilience the ability to recover from or adjust to change

sadist a person who likes being cruel

sagely wisely

suspend to hang or to stop temporarily

swivet extreme nervousness or worry

systole something that closes regularly, like a heart valve

tangible able to be understood by touch

tesseract in the fourth dimension, the equivalent of a cube

tractable obedient or easily influenced

Mrs. Who uses quotes throughout *A Wrinkle in Time* because she has trouble expressing herself in her own words. The quotes are also a good way to introduce readers to other writers they may not have heard of before. The quotes and traditional sayings are always short and illustrate a point in the story. Here is a list of all the quotations used in *A Wrinkle in Time.*

CHAPTER 2

Pascal
Le coeur a ses raisons que la raison ne connait point. (French)
The heart has its reasons, whereof reason knows nothing.

Traditional saying
Auf frischer Tat ertappt (German)
In flagrante delicto (Latin)
Caught in the act (English)

Seneca
Ab honesto virum bonum nihil deterret. (Latin)
Nothing deters a good man from doing what is honorable.

Traditional saying

Justitiae soror fides. (Latin)

Faith is the sister of justice.

CHAPTER 3

Dante

Come t'è picciol fallo amaro morso! (Italian)

What grievous pain a little fault doth give thee!

A Perez

Un asno viejo sabe más que un potro. (Spanish)

An old ass knows more than a young colt.

CHAPTER 4

Horace

Finxerunt animi, raro et perpauca loquentis. (Latin)

To action little, less to words inclined.

Euripedes

Αεηπου οὐδὲν, πὰντα δ' εηπίζειυ χρεωτ. (Greek)

Nothing is hopeless; we must hope for everything.

Traditional saying

Qui plus sait, plus se tait. (French)

The more a man knows, the less he talks.

Traditional saying

Vitam impendere vero. (Latin)

To stake one's life for the truth.

Traditional saying

Das Werk lobt den Meister. (German)

The work proves the craftsman.

CHAPTER 5

Cervantes

La experiencia es la madre de la ciencia. (Spanish)

Experience is the mother of knowledge.

Shakespeare

We are such stuff as dreams are made on.

Prospero in *The Tempest*

Delille

Que la terre est petite à qui la voit des cieux! (French)

How small is the earth to him who looks from heaven.

Bible

And the light shineth in darkness; and the darkness
   comprehended it not.

CHAPTER 6

Traditional saying

As paredes tem ouvidos. (Portuguese)

Walls have ears.

Goethe

Allwissend bin ich nicht; doch viel ist mir bewisst. (German)

I do not know everything; still many things I understand.

When she was five years old, Madeleine L'Engle wrote her first story, which, she remembers, wasn't very good. She was in the fifth grade when she first tried writing a novel. She loved writing and continued to write as she grew up.

As a child, L'Engle was sent to boarding school, where she was never very popular as a result of her shy, introspective manner. L'Engle recalls, "I learned to put on protective coloring in order to survive in an atmosphere which was alien; and I learned to concentrate. . . . The result of this early lesson in concentration is that I can write anywhere."

Though L'Engle has written more than fifty books in her career—poetry, journals, plays, fiction, and nonfiction—she hasn't always had an easy time writing. As a young wife and mother in Connecticut, she often had very little time to write, so she decided to stop. She tried not writing but couldn't help herself. She describes what happened: "I had to write. I had no choice in the matter. It was not up to me to say I would stop, because I could not. It didn't matter how small or inadequate my talent. If I never had another book published, and it was very clear to me that this was a real possibility, I still had to go on writing."

"Kids ask me where I get my ideas from and I tell them that ideas are everywhere—the trick is learning to recognize them."

Reading is one way of finding new ideas for stories. L'Engle reads constantly, and especially enjoys reading about science.

"One physicist says that the big question is: Are we alone in the universe or not?" That question has inspired Madeleine L'Engle to explore the cosmos and to think about life on other planets, in other universes.

L'Engle says that she tries to tell a story that is more than just a story. "I am not interested in telling a story that merely entertains." She goes on to say that "stories have a richness that goes way beyond fact. My writing knows more than I know. What a writer must do is listen to her book. It might take you where you don't expect to go. That's what happens when you write stories. You listen and you say 'aha,' and you write it down. A lot of it is not planned, not conscious; it happens while you're doing it. You know more about it after you're done."

But first, how does one start? L'Engle has a simple formula: "I start with what I know with all five senses, what I have experienced, and then the imagination takes over and says, 'But what if—' and the story is on."

L'Engle is skilled at keeping readers interested and wanting to read more. "One of the things a storyteller really has to know how to do is to make you want to find out what is going to happen next, make you want to turn the page."

L'Engle acknowledges that she writes first and foremost for herself. "I write for me. I think that is when we are at our best, when we can tell something that is a struggle within us, its questions, its problems. We work it out through our craft."

She says that one of the things she likes best about writing is that "when there are problems in a book, I can resolve them. In life it's not so easy."

Someone once asked her if she was writing anything at the moment and L'Engle replied, "Of course I'm writing something now. I'm not nice when I'm not writing."

- **A new chapter:** Start a story of your own using a last line from one of the chapters. Here are a few to choose from:

  "The tesseract—" Mrs. Murry whispered. "What did she mean? How could she have known?"

  "That dark Thing we saw," she said. "Is that what my father is fighting?"

  "I can't stand it any longer," she sobbed. "Watch now, children, watch!"

  "I've got another feeling. Not the same kind, a different one, a feeling that if we go into that building we're going into terrible danger."

  Meg grabbed wildly at Calvin, shrieking, "That isn't Charles! Charles is gone!"

- Write a story that begins or ends with one of the quotations in the book and that illustrates the point of the quote. For example, "Walls have ears." What might happen in a story that started—or ended—that way?

- **Nobody's perfect:** Make a list of your own faults. How do your faults hold you back? How could these same faults help you? Then, write a story about a person with your faults. In the story, let the character learn to recognize her or his faults and maybe find a way to overcome them or use them.

• **Character sketch:** Mrs. Whatsit is a pretty odd character. Make up your own odd character. Write a few paragraphs clearly describing the person's clothes, behavior, and speech.

• **Meg's diary:** Write a diary entry that Meg might write before her adventure. Write another entry for her after she returns.

• **Fast forward:** Charles Wallace is an extraordinary child. What do you think Charles Wallace will be like when he grows up? Describe him.

• **A planet just for you:** Make up your own planet in another galaxy. Describe the setting and the creatures that live there. What is life like on your imaginary world? What do the inhabitants believe is good and what do they think is evil?

- **Quotations as decorations:** Pick your favorite quote from the book. Using craft paper and colored pens, write the quote in your best handwriting—or use block letters—and hang it on your wall.

- **Create your own wrinkle:** Think of two objects that are far apart. Using a long sheet of paper, make a drawing of one of them at one end of the paper. At the opposite end, draw the other. Now, draw a line connecting the two things. Next, fold the paper so that the two objects are side by side. See how the folds—or wrinkles—bring the two objects together.

- **Heroes:** Two of Madeleine L'Engle's personal heroes are Johann Sebastian Bach and Albert Einstein. When she wrote *A Wrinkle in Time*, L'Engle hoped Meg would be a hero to those who read the book. Make a list of your favorite heroes. Think about why they are your heroes and what they have done for the world. What could you do to make a difference?

- **Act it out:** *A Wrinkle in Time* is filled with exciting dialogue and wonderful action scenes. Pick a section from the book and act it out with friends. You could even dress like one of the characters from the book.

T he series titles are grouped in the order in which they should be read, not the order in which they were written. *An Acceptable Time* is sometimes included as part of the O'Keefe Family series and sometimes as the fifth book in the Time Quartet. It is included with the O'Keefe Family series here, since it is about Meg's daughter Polly O'Keefe.

Other *A Wrinkle in Time* books by Madeleine L'Engle

Murry Family series:

A Wind in the Door (1973)

A Swiftly Tilting Planet (1978)

Many Waters (1986)

Other series by Madeleine L'Engle

O'Keefe Family series:

The Arm of the Starfish (1965)

Dragons in the Water (1976)

A House Like a Lotus (1984)

An Acceptable Time (1989)

Austin Family series:

The Twenty-Four Days Before Christmas (1984)

A Full House: An Austin Family Christmas (1999)

Meet the Austins (Vanguard Press, 1960; Farrar, Straus & Giroux, 1997)

The Anti-Muffins (1980)
The Moon by Night (1963)
The Young Unicorns (1968)
A Ring of Endless Light (1980)
Troubling a Star (1994)

Katherine Forrester Vigneras series:
The Small Rain (Vanguard Press, 1945; Farrar, Straus & Giroux, 1984)
A Severed Wasp (1982)

Camilla Dickinson series:
Camilla Dickinson (Simon & Schuster 1951; Delacorte Press, 1981)
A Live Coal in the Sea (1996)

Other books by Madeleine L'Engle
And Both Were Young (Lothrop, Lee & Shepard Co., 1949; Bantam Doubleday Dell, 1983)
The Journey with Jonah (1967, 1971)
Dance in the Desert (1969)
Ladder of Angels: Scenes from the Bible Illustrated by Children of the World (Harper & Row, 1979; Penguin, 1980)
The Sphinx at Dawn: Two Stories (1982)
The Glorious Impossible: Jesus Christ and His Family (1990)
The Other Dog (2001)

Bibliography

Books

Commire, Anne. *Something About the Author*. Vol. 1, pp.141–142.
Detroit: Gale Research Company, 1971.

L'Engle, Madeleine. *Herself*. Colorado Springs, Colo.: Shaw, 2001.

Newquist, Roy. *Conversations*. New York: Rand McNally, 1967.

Telgen, Diane, ed. *Something About the Author*. Vol. 75,
pp.114–121. Detroit: Gale Research Inc., 1994.

Magazines

Children's Literature in Education. Summer 1976, pp. 96–102;
winter 1983, pp. 195–203l; spring 1987, pp. 34–44.

Christian Century, April 6, 1977, p. 321.

Hearne, Betsy. "A Mind in Motion: A Few Moments with
Madeleine L'Engle," *School Library Journal*. Vol. 44, No. 6, June
1998, pp. 28–33.

Horowitz, Shel. "The Story on Truth and Fact," *Writer's Digest*,
April 1992, p. 6.

L'Engle, Madeleine. "Do I Dare Disturb the Universe?" *Horn Book
Magazine*. Vol. 59, No. 6, December 1983, pp. 673–682.

———. "The Expanding Universe: Newbery Award Acceptance,"
Horn Book Magazine. Vol. 39, No. 4, August 1963, pp. 351–355.

National Catholic Reporter. June 20, 1986, p. 9; November 17,
1989, p. 30.

School Library Journal. Vol. 44, No. 6, June 1998, pp. 28–33.

Web sites

American Catholic:

www.americancatholic.org/Messenger/Jun2000/feature1.asp

American Library Association:

www.ala.org/news/archives/v3n11/v3n11c.html

Educational Paperback Association:

www.edupaperback.org/authorbios/L'Engle_Madeleine. html

Frugal Fun:

www.frugalfun.com/l'engle.html

Internet Pub Library:

www.ipl.org/youth/AskAuthor

KidsReads, part of The Book Report Network:

www.kidsreads.com/series/series-time-author.asp

Sweet Briar College, Gifts of Speech; Women's Speeches from Around the World:

http://gos.sbc.edu/l/lengle.html

TeenReads, part of The Book Report Network:

www.teenreads.com/authors/au-lengle-madeleine.asp